01

Blueprint for Life   ISBN 0-9536958-2-4

Written by Ray Hollingsworth
Photography and design by Lee Thomas

www.cultpoet.co.uk   www.erotic-cafe.net
e-mail; erotic.cafe@btopenworld.com

Available through amazon.co.uk and all leading
retailers in the UK and Europe

Previous Titles
The Erotic Cafe 1999   ISBN 0-9536958-0-8
The Pornstar and the Priest 2001   ISBN 0-9536958-1-6

Printed by Jenner (City Print) Ltd

Published by Kiss Production Limited 2004

Front cover image
Model, Nicola Floyd
Photography by Clive Austen
Courtesy of The Attitude Model Agency

contents

This stuff has been written on location in the UK. I'm not sure if what I do can be described as poetry. I write it as I see it and as I feel it. I do not edit the work. Sorry to purists, but I do not believe in structure or form. I do not believe in creative writing classes. I do not believe in using a thesaurus.

I write fast and I live with the results. Hopefully anyone that reads 'Blueprint' will get something from it. If you are a writer yourself then the only advice I can offer is, do what comes naturally. Listen to no one.

Thank you to Lee Thomas for the images and design. Lee also worked on 'The Erotic Café' and 'The Pornstar and the Priest'. Thank you to everyone that has supported my work over the last few years.

Ray Hollingsworth.

Droplets

running down skin

on the beach   transistor tunes in

multi-electrode valves crackle

bad news travels fast

in the heat

acting on a tip off

police broke in to a room in a guest house

a gramaphone purchased 48 hours earlier

repeating a line from a sixties' single

by Billy Fury

a bloodstained doll

with the head torn off

she always wanted to be famous

today her face

a digital self portrait

seen simultaneously on 15 news channels

and on line

should make tomorrow's papers

and posters will appear on ice cream kiosks

in the penny arcade   at the railway station

and be seen by

school teachers   and day trippers

and those that had a casual fling

no one ever got close

down by the promenade

she's cut off all her hair

watches the clouds

and sings 'Halfway to Paradise'

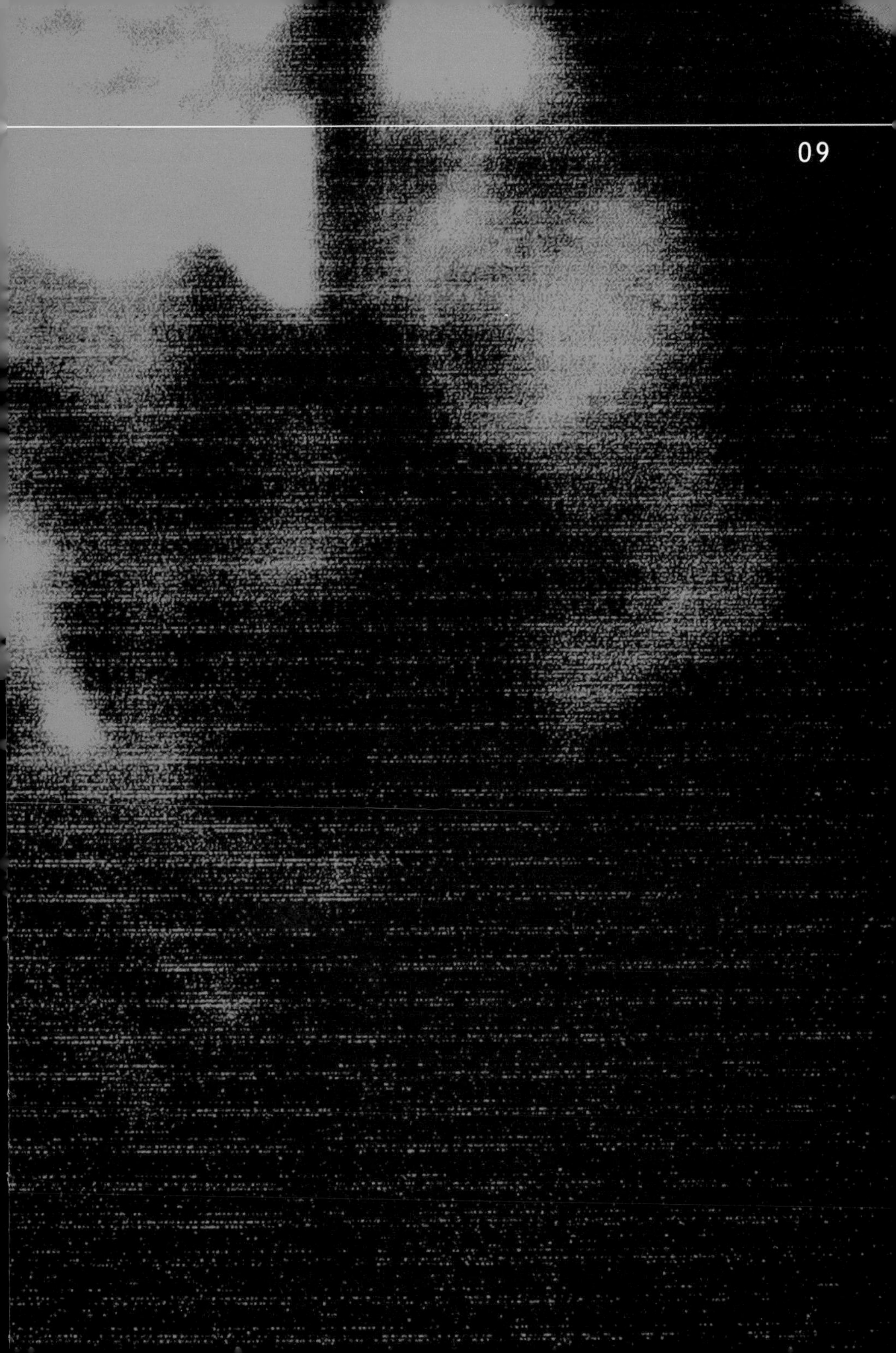

Innate and intuitive senses

sparkle in the morning

thoughts dissolving   water on tissue

on up escalators

moving through silent noise

transparent capsules float

in the atmosphere

account executives

between Buckhurst Hill and Tottenham Court Road

in silent space   the idea implodes

something   from another time zone

a concept on a cellphone

last night's love was a disappointment

tonight it's back to the bar

Think product

think retail

something you heard on a tv programme

a trendy word

for once   standing alone

you see a stranger

the one from the film

the one in four dreams you had last week

in cheap hotels

follow her down a corridor

and into a room

the lighting in pop videos has a lot to answer for

the only evidence that it happened

the soluble contact lens in your pocket

love was blazed across car windscreens   on the M6

dancers from seedy joints in the West Midlands

cavorted in cages   dangled on cables

suspended from blue cranes 80ft high

prismatic colours

bursting through cellophane

compliant to

harmonised standards

the strip light flickers

a taxi turns in the drive

we're moving pictures

touch helps us to survive

Your celtic breath

the weightlessness

touch and turn   we can't see tomorrow

it happened quickly

at the petrol station   always easier

passing hours   measured somewhere

not here

we're radio equipment   feeding static

electromagnetic compatibility

the day job gives us

nothing

the neighbourhood decay

media is empty

just say you'll stay

at least through the weekend

laying in a foetal position

i draw around you in charcoal

i'll pin the sheet to the wall

on Monday morning

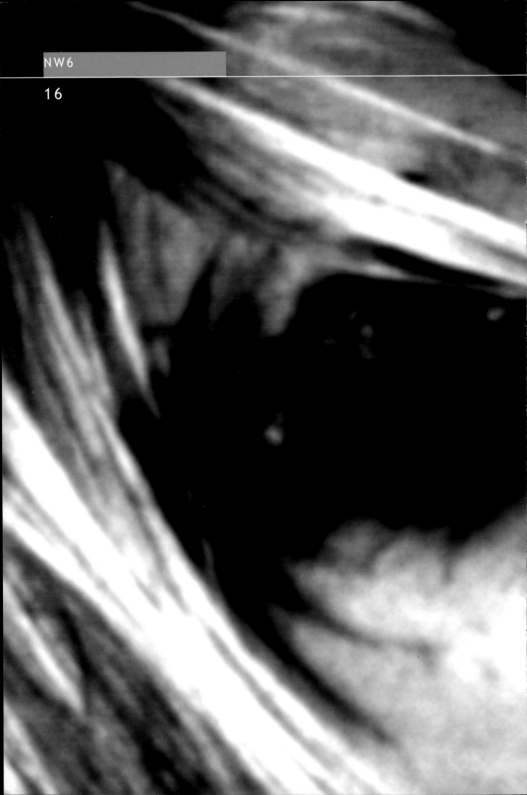

In kilburn

the desert moonlight

alluring but cruel

entices our souls

an act that connects us

momentarily frozen

our very existence

we are the unborn

tonight we recapture

in a sepia dream

burning raw incense

a closeness so pure

our transient spirit

above and beyond

this neon metropolis

where we all sold out

Taking in   information

feel the static in the air

you could be someone   I could be anyone

does anyone really care

to a concrete-lit domain   postcards from Berlin

taste the sulphur in the rain   sleek lines

and textured skin

this city steals our souls   style in overkill

moving atoms   making patterns

image is everything

the rush relayed on plasma screen

super slomo   edit cut

on line magazine

20 simple movements kit   factor 8 at speed of light

self indulged   anaesthetised

chrome reflects the night

touching your skin   and breathing you in

this is Canada Water

I know you're out there

somewhere

late-night shopping people hopping

once I thought I saw you

at a street café

drawing zen pictures in the afternoon

your pink lipstick message on a mirror

it always haunted me

it still does

the seventy five point seven calls

from your cocaine bed

out your head

the frozen state that you became

a drowning flame

those people that you knew

the select few

I don't think so

I always harboured the idea

of some kind of twilight rescue

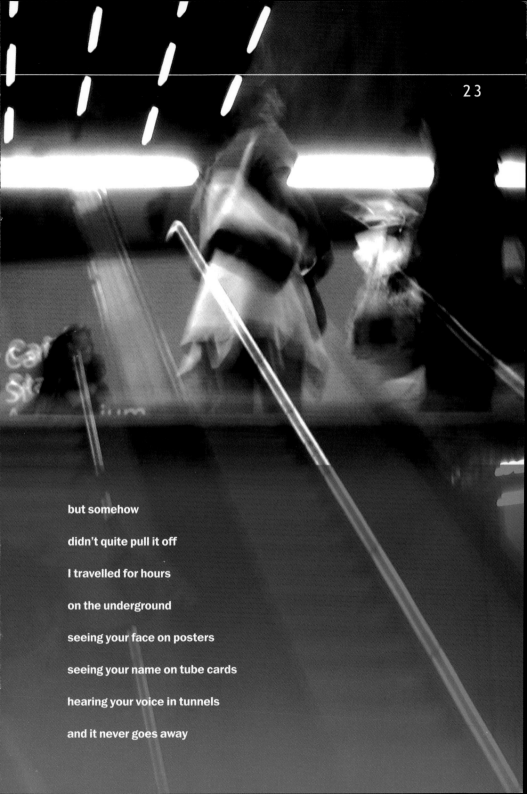

but somehow

didn't quite pull it off

I travelled for hours

on the underground

seeing your face on posters

seeing your name on tube cards

hearing your voice in tunnels

and it never goes away

oh and yes

I lit ten thousand candles for you

in a dream

so you could say

that doesn't count

but surely

it tells you something

and your silhouette

I saw it projected on buildings

in Canary Wharf

I saw it in the night skies

over Lewisham

I loved the blue streaks in you hair

the sound of your footsteps

on the stairs

and your black dress

it still hangs

in my wardrobe

Your heart's a stolen car

speeding through some cocktail bar

the night's amphetamine

the flightpath of transmitted dreams

some pose of confidence

programmed intrigue and suspense

the lambs are never far

stand in the shadows of your star

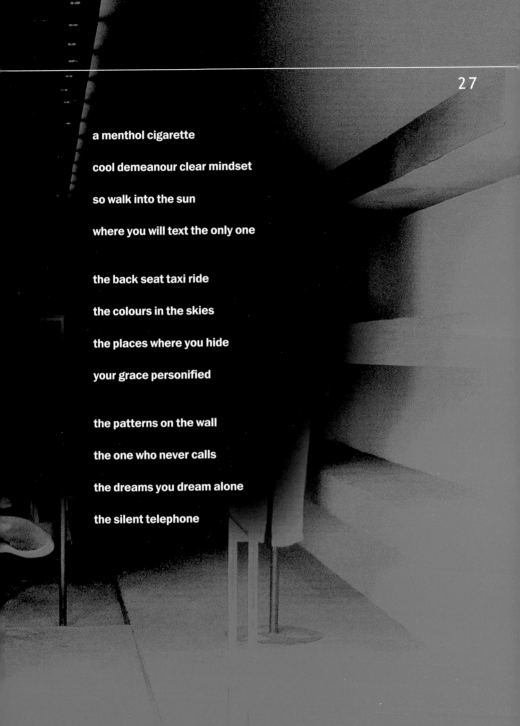

a menthol cigarette

cool demeanour clear mindset

so walk into the sun

where you will text the only one

the back seat taxi ride

the colours in the skies

the places where you hide

your grace personified

the patterns on the wall

the one who never calls

the dreams you dream alone

the silent telephone

Don't feed the pigeons

you know it always makes you cry

keep out of the sunlight

don't walk under the sky

keep away from sources of ignition

including pilot lights and sparks

avoid going out at night

into the ghetto of broken hearts

avoid prolonged or repeated contact with skin

it may be harmful to unleash what lays within

you are a pressurised container

which should not be exposed

to temperatures above 50°c

you may be harmful if inhaled

vapours can ignite

explosively

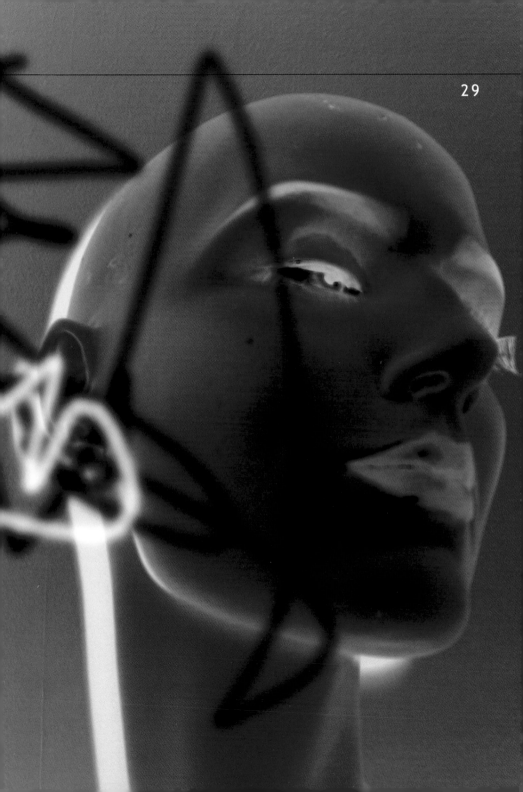

And so to altered state in timeless space

reflecting colours so far unseen

encrypted language from some distant dream

float we through modern city

over what is deemed to be

and unmistakably is ordinary life

numb to sight and sound

but lifted to some higher ground

this is eternal   this is meant to be

how do we comprehend the incomprehensible

though we try we are unable

never wake us   never take us from this moment

spontaneity   a split-second changes everything

yes

deliver

we are delivered

in Portland Square you shimmered

numb

entranced

running like the wind

you danced

in shadows

Your psyche wielding its way

up the staircase onto the landing

bathes in the sunrays   diffuses scent

splays ten years of memory

in the microbe dust atmosphere

some lurid pose

virgin bitch   whore goddess

in swirling musk

biker speeds off in shadow world

blasting rock   leaking fuel

the kebab shop angel calls

six digit cab numbers   debris decorates the day

the headset still playing on the spot where he lay

talk to me baby   rise up and walk away

think of us in that shabby bedsit

getting high on cola and love

fish and chips off newspapers   the run down pubs

a utopian heaven   if only

if only we could tell them

the ambulance arrived   the skies all florescent

the earth pulsating   lifting us above the hollow

mourners pouring out their grief

from the tower of st. stephens the colours of the flowers beneath

lighting up this drab town

I'm coming round again   to see you in all your glory

in the cracked mirror   by the sash window

above the kerb and the gutter

where it all happens   the dog ends and the beer cans

the slaughter of the innocent

want you to be the one   that I remember in ten thousand years

clear as yesterday   clear as now

your head jerking backwards   honey milk fusion

moving dynamics   shadowplay illusion

heard about twenty five layers of paint on some car

saw the loose change in your coffee jar

know where I would rather be

press yourself against me in this film

in the cut the skies are all florescent

push yourself against me in this dream

the beginning and the end and everything between

34

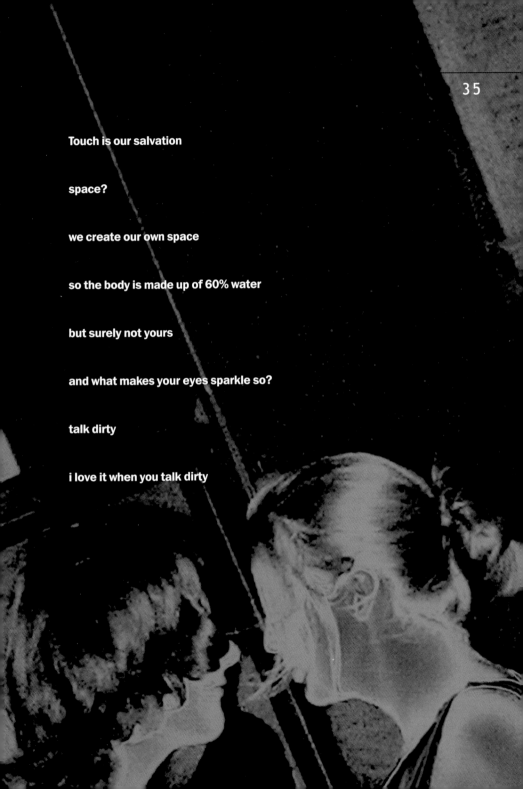

Touch is our salvation

space?

we create our own space

so the body is made up of 60% water

but surely not yours

and what makes your eyes sparkle so?

talk dirty

i love it when you talk dirty

Last thing I remember   you dancing in the tail lights

in leopard skin shoes   in a hotel carpark

the high octave living   your heart did a u-turn

you leaving with friends   or was it with him

at the time I was shaken   friends rallied round

on a sofa in chelsea   licking my wounds

I never recovered   for the rest of the summer

or the summers that followed

and you only human

a girl like you   happens once in a lifetime

can it really happen that often?

40

Once   caught in a lens

from a fourth floor balcony

breathless   wreckless

rebel flesh   writhing

love is a message on a waiting room wall

scrawled in eyeliner

closer   straight to detail   words failed

walking in the rain on Saturday

staring at strangers

feeling pain   but blameless

this tide washes over   cleanses no one

returns unannounced   years later

lens extends   your words   life is a drive through

hurt tears us apart   oblivious

turning the pages of a magazine

disguised as lifestyle

unable to look   at your face

your face is beautiful

especially when anger sets in

personality moodswing

the small scar   noticed second time   at little venice

I knew then just like I know now

on the table

keys   a carton of orange juice   body spray

everything is you

hair unfurled   I wanted to keep you

from the world

things are happening   down on the street

on this screen   it all goes over   it all goes through us

trust

a word I found in your filofax

once

we are minute detail

dust

soft focus

but always there

just

Meet me at dawn in a seedy hotel

live out the scene that you know so well

kick off your shoes peel off your dress

let's light the fuse and rip up some flesh

hiss spit and snarl rip the cord from the wall

tighten your grip mistreat and control

a semi skilled worker you're certainly not

a five star deserter from the eastern block

the pleasure the poison it's a very fine line

we measure the poison by the heat at the time

Stepping out

into this land

of shrink wrapped bottle blondes

ringtones and logos

where pillow talk is cheap

and it's 9 below zero

I think of a time

when I longed for you to call

only yesterday

I saw a man staring in the deep freeze

punch drunk by cardboard meals for one

tonight

moonlit profiles rush by

in a flicker book of dreams

that never happen

odd particles of consumer durables

scattered in this doorway

where we got burned in the flames

now

only silence remains

alleyway lights on dimmers

housewives scan ads for slimmers

and girls that taste of perfume

gaze into ikea mirrors

a pink loveheart crushed on the laminate

at flat 14a

By the neon machine

inserting tokens treading in lights

latin eyes spell sensual

energy provided by NPower

special tarrifs apply after 11.30pm

the kind of tourist

who squeezes every last drop

from the sachet

living the illusion

pinned against a damp plaster wall

takes it in her stride

watches people passing by

a flash photo for private viewing

away from ringtones

some touch

it was like someone turned off the world

it could have been the last day of her life

I don't remember hearing the trains

go over the bridge

scent in the fabric

every move recorded

these minutes ticking by

displayed in florescent

Neff green

short stories of love

eyes roll

textures

remember this

how it destroys

eats at the senses

this surrender

I glanced your way

you danced away

over the table tops

and through a hole in the sky

reflections

of your gaze

trailblazed

make us feel that we can fly

walking the sleepy leafy streets in sunshine

it's your time

I'm snowblind

into the slipsteam

the street signs say sublime

each incandescent millisecond

etched in time

your glow

blown

on the line

this city is no shrine

unguided pathway to the sun

the filmset of this lifetime

the paper vendor

the taxi driver

and this place

do not exist

and the turning on the corner

it is mist

burning eyes

feel inspired

falling hopelessly

through timeless

space

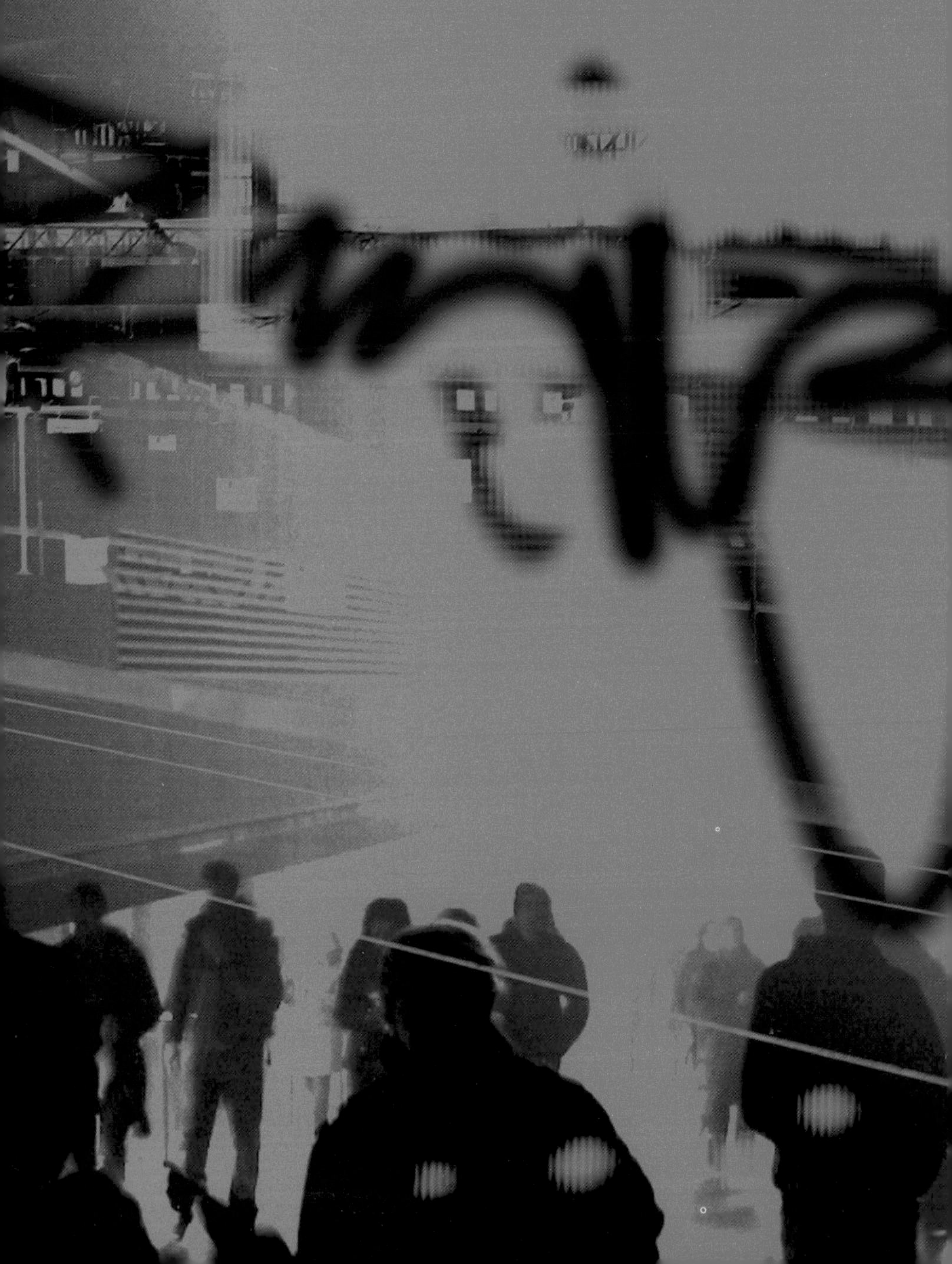

It must have been the angle of sunlight
or something
from no more than 2 feet away
she was leaning forward
applying lipstick
I looked into her eyes
and through the other side
a boarded up newsagents
and litter burned the surface of the road
stolen cars passed by
I'm holding a menu and I'm disengaged

in her 2 inch heels
I imagine the soundtrack of footsteps
echoes deflect   off cranes at the docks
as an executive turns his car engine off
silver wires   on an ink blue photograph
processed moments earlier
at the all night chemist
by the all night café
24 hour cutting edge   as it happens...

and in the restaurant
the scouse sort   in the tight black dress
gets up from the table   at last
watched by the waiter   and any other that dares
a newspaper   on the counter says
' Mum dead in blaze '
A YOUNG mum died and her baby daughter and husband
were injured when fire tore through their home today.

Firefighters pulled the woman from the flames but were
unable to save her.
West Brom 1 Everton 2
TWO MEN JAILED who stabbed a care worker to death
and left him to die in the street have both been jailed
Jersey – cruise and fly
UNIT MANAGER (Project Delivery)
£23,358 to £24,726
Our Beautiful Grand-daughter is 18 today
Top school must close
CAVERN CLUB 1957, 1961, '62 or '63 membership cards wanted
N REG ESCORT TD 1.8 LX £1250 o.n.o.

Posters were peeling off the hoardings
cans strewn across grass verges
where office workers engaged in tacky conversations
and the streets were aglow
with shellsuits and midriffs
it's been a long hot day in the city
on every street corner there are signs

Meet in a public place
Inform a friend of your whereabouts
Do not accept a lift home (however kind the offer)
Do not give out your address until you are ready
Stay in control...

60

And so to the twilight world
where street lights glow
and Peugeots float   in a sleazy haze
in the distance   out of the blue mist
a forlorn figure waves
to a varied section of society
cruising at 15mph
others are lurking
extras with walk-on parts
in an underworld   being filmed
by a freelance production crew   all in view
of security guards   moving cards
at the bulk container depot
discussing the likely contents   of cheap designer handbags
an insight into this world   soon to be exposed
by Damien Hirst   at an exhibition in the south
held in four dissused aeroplane hangars
in close proximity to   a convienient turn off
on the M25...

a former housewife   now an insomniac
pores over small ads in the early hours
and contemplates how she wrote to an agony aunt
at a PO Box number in Chorley
'we still have sex but we rarely kiss, it is all very abrupt,
less like love and more like lust. It isn't enough I have
to be needed Christine...'
now she has a new life where the concept of
everlasting love does not exist...

Toyah drinks from a chipped Mr Man mug
at a formica table with coffee stains
and last night's remains   of paranoia in an ashtray
she surveys the manikin bus queue
their glass eyes glazed and frozen
since the last episode of
the Patrick McGowan thing with the giant bubble
burnt out cars line the horizon
and the garages in the block
where the doors are ripped off
seep battery acid and poison
aerosol stencil graphics depict gas masks
smeared on street signs and walls
even over a Roni Size poster
while rats pillage bins down at the school
the next generation are spat out
on the landscape arriving in recycled buggies
courtesy of Mothercare one has a wheel missing
a mother tells her grizzling son to
'shut the fuck up you little bastard'
another sports a black eye and an array of lovebites
possibly the work of more than one partner
and throws down a dog end in the gutter

there is excitement in the air   tonight is talent spotting
in the Bull n Bear   last week a sort got nutted
at the top of the stairs   near the fag machine
some little slag   from the rollerhockey team
and Madonna singing ' Ray of Light '
was hit full in the gob   by a steak n kidney pie
and a few chips for good measure
take your pleasure   this is   modern city living…

64

at the end of the bus route kids shoot
at corporation personel wearing bullet-proof clothing
funded by council tax contributions that never get paid
word has it there's just been a raid at the laundrette
two duvet covers and four flanlette sheets
speed off in a Vauxhall Chevette
with a broken windscreen...

Kevin had a history of violence the report said
used to keep breadknives and barbed wire in his bed
pictures of criminals on the living room wall
a collection of blunt instuments
from the scene of crimes in his chest of drawers
'ad temper tantrams when e was two   and it got
fuckin worse   his step brother 6 an in an earse
e let out a scream   that was eard fa miles
people say they can still ear it now   10 years on
e developed this craze fa edbuttin people
fuckin anyone that came near   the window cleaner
the postman   an that woman cross road
the one that never spoke   he fuckin caught er one night
she needed dentures   think she ad to go into
an home   then there was these people turned up
one mornin   said somfing bout some therapy
an experiment they said   been tried in New Zealand
a tape recording of fuckin wilderbeasts givin birth
or summit   told em ta fuck off at firs
e was monitered by a panel of specialists
white coats they ad   e seemed ta reach a sense of calm

they were really pleased with the progress   but then Kevin
tried to bite off someone's arm   a couple of weeks lata I get this letta
sayin that they were recommending Kevin be considered for
a career as a social worker...

I WANNA be able to walk around with no clothes on
and have a bath with the door open on a double decker bus
I WANNA see that programme tonight about
Lithuania liberating America...

It's been a long hot day in the city
posters were peeling off hoardings
midriffs were showing
glad I got that number

Through the blinds   in aphonic night

the girl with the silver car   and the tip up lights

on a telepathic highway   to the moon and dreams beyond

a subliminal co-existence   an indefinable bond

shoot stars into the kitchen   we are seven centuries on

wires transmit a message   tyres decipher code

her pixelated image   our data contraflow

Who else would phone at 2am

and talk about nothing for nearly two hours

and yet strangely hold my attention

Christ six years and not a word

who else would demand cigarettes and wine

'we could talk of old times'

forever the insomniac it seems

while all around you are lost in dreams

in timeless night I duly succumb

driving across town

the traffic lights seem redundant

milk floats rule the highway

council workers clean the streets of blood

and fast food debris

ghostly figures grope in a doorway

police car tail lights seem more pronounced

how will I find you

will you still be five feet two

will your hair still be blonde

will you still smell of summer rain

and do you still drive fast round corners

I kept your Christmas card and your note

I remember how you smoked in bed

but somehow

it didn't seem to matter

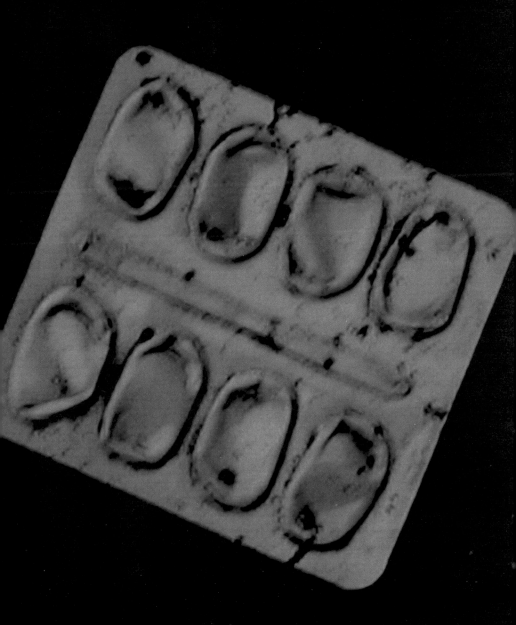

You come around here with your wild party eyes

love is pure   we made it that way

don't want to see you for days

but will think of you always   all ways

don't phone for weeks

let the tension mount on the streets

it's passion that counts

in the heat of the moment

we'll break and take all

we make the rules

in the cyclone moan falling to the floor

I'll be walking along the sea front and listening to the roar

love lasts forever

when we're not together

Here she comes

dressed in flesh

the blue star

by the left eye

upstairs there's a better view

an idea in foil

for safe keeping

later dropped

at Odeon Screen One

walking home

a playing card face down

played on the mind

living inside an illusion

Tuesday came

an image seen

of a girl writing a journal

in a squat

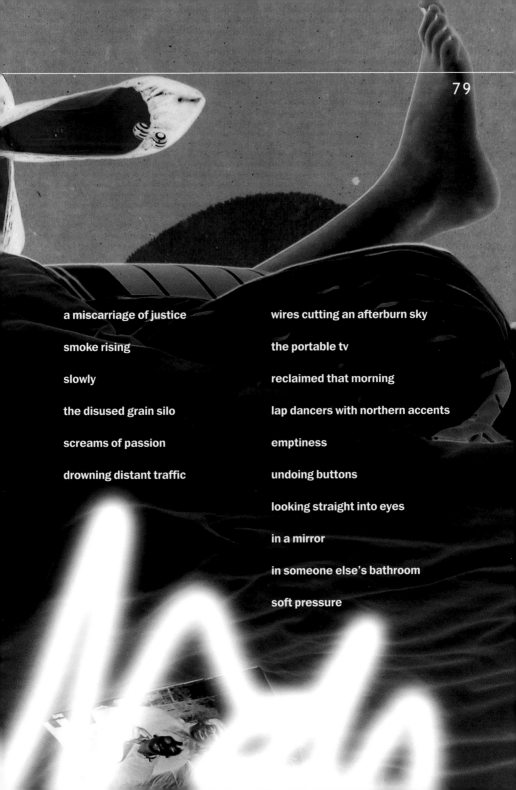

a miscarriage of justice

smoke rising

slowly

the disused grain silo

screams of passion

drowning distant traffic

wires cutting an afterburn sky

the portable tv

reclaimed that morning

lap dancers with northern accents

emptiness

undoing buttons

looking straight into eyes

in a mirror

in someone else's bathroom

soft pressure

self exerted

going downstairs for the kill

a remote blip

changes channels

the doctrine of some German philosopher

forever engrained

there is no god

there is no right or wrong

there is no reason to living

the only certainty in life

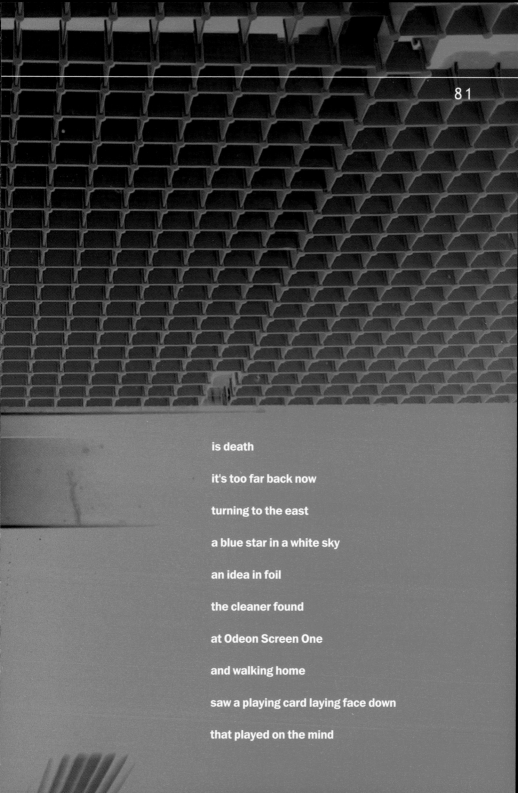

is death

it's too far back now

turning to the east

a blue star in a white sky

an idea in foil

the cleaner found

at Odeon Screen One

and walking home

saw a playing card laying face down

that played on the mind

Enter

the sleazy soda stream princess

(that was some kind of entrance)

the non-restricted access in navy and denim

turn on the meter in pulsating neon

take the injection and know what's coming

you

you're so judgemental and you're going

nowhere

we can hear your eyes move

assassin

voyeur

Cutting through this air, transfixed

we are trading light, creating mood

we gate crash heaven, in through the back door

enticed by an illegal substance packaged as instinct

outside there is a war of attrition

street fighters rape the highway

delivered by Sky News to our microcosm living spaces

our species in a permanent state of numbness

for someone else's commercial gain

sleep twenty four seven

but us, just for now

time travellers

there must be a name for it

the great escape or something

living for the moment maybe

me, I don't believe in life after death

here and now we do this thing

there is nothing else

86

The small print in the disclaimer could be coming into play here

the final countdown to the seventh coming when we rearrange things

the smoke is rising, takes an age to hit the moon

felt the warmth inside but could be out of here soon

we've been treading eggshells for five weeks or more now

communicating in some kind of code

looking out at separate horizons, walking on two different roads

eat food look out of the window

thought waves are black type on the front page

if this is the end then I'm glad it begun

'cause I was no one until there was you

fifty reasons why we can't happen

an imbalance of lifestyles, deep rooted extremes

turn out the lights turn on the passion

haunts us forever repeated in dreams

we've been through big talk and small talk

your ice blue eyes melted me more than times you could ever know

You and I

we know why we're here

a pact

some mutual understanding

an unwritten law

we will get out before recrimination

there will be no open wounds

no walking past the high rise

through splintered glass

we will not drive stakes through hearts

not us

night will melt into morning

GMTV that stark reminder of this nothingness

just for a moment

layed bare before us

caught off guard

as body mist drifts in brilliant sunlight

this is where it gets tough

you and I

we know why we're here

this is us

high altitude flying

was always going to be our downfall

on recall

images emerging from shadows

by day and by night

people say that time heals

but us

we know how it feels

could have fallen for you

looking like that in the shower

but we're not going back

to where we've been before

we are tough

resilient

and we still have time for religion

or alternative living

we're up with giving

and laying in the debris

of another aftermath

So tonight will you sellotape my soul to your Vauxhall Vectra

will you sell my heart to a nervous bidder

will you invade the chambers of my innermost secrets

and scatter them on commuters at King's Cross station

will you tell me you love me then turn to another

will you do what you do under the covers

will you breathe fire like the very first night

will you walk the wire in high heels and black tights

and I learned to write your name like you write your name

with the curly bit on the d

was this obsession or was it junk tv

so are we in love or are we a habit

i remember you saying expect the unexpected

and you always lived up to your promises

and who else will meet you on an underground station

and ask for your name and number

you said it was fate

I said it was my left side talking

the train was late and when we went walking

we were flying

The tear drop in the headlights

some phantom in the skies

a desolation angel

a Mondeo drifting by

the girl with the two tone hair

on a poster for a picture show

someone cried tonight

on the last bus home

standing in the shadows

lonely by the cash machine

a water colour rainbow

faded mascara, denim jeans

a black and white fiim

at the tv rental

Paris 62

mood experimental

hey you

yeah you

in the pink skirt and black tights

baby blue eyes

you're gonna miss

your flight

Angels run wild in the streets

sensors react to body heat

neons shine as digital time

moves closer to midnight

girls clock boys eye to eye

senses on high

front cover face

pulses race

and lovers embrace

in the subway

faces with no name

faces in freeze frame

get closer and closer

perfume fills the air

the casual glance

a moment to share

contact is made

but in a second it fades

and is gone forever

car wheels burn

as young hearts turn

to love in the fast lane

temperature rises tension ignites

the streets are on fire

in electric night

as the last record plays

contact is made

closer and closer

hand touches hand

skin touches skin

a new lifetime begins

then the lights come on

and they are gone

forever

street lights glow

as night clubs close

and people drift home

angels rest their heads

in suburbia beds

and dream of tomorrow

100

Cigarette still burning   your perfume fills the room

the curtains are back   you've been gazing at the moon

tonight I hear a voice   it rebounds off the stars

you created distance   you created time

you created space   you were never mine

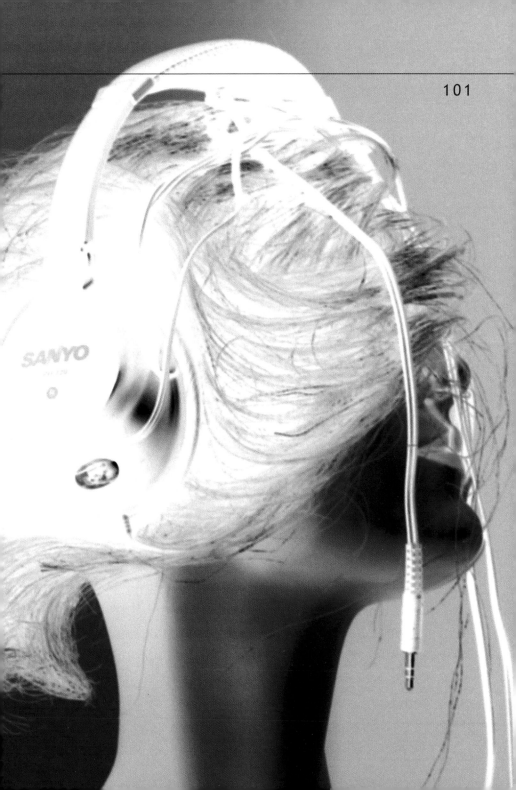

Chaotic scenes

as face and body pierced monsters

from a northern town in outer space

shout abuse and grapple with interbred scum

from high rise slums in tinsel town

this is Britain

don't go out when the lights go down

a barrage of low cost loan

if you own your own home commercials

fired non-stop tracer bullet-like

this is entertainment

or exploitation of fucking idiots

it depends which way you look at it

the television's on

the television's never off

it's riveting stuff

a gameshow where the contestants all have

one thing in common

they're ugly

and not only this

some are five foot one

and some are six foot six

the television's on

despite a power cut

generators provided by corporate advertisers

are outside near the telephone masts

I once heard of a man in Sheffield

who used to shag his wife

over the back of a DFS settee

while he ate a bacon sandwich

and watched tv

Fords thrashed   Astras crashed and suicide plights   housewives bashed

schoolgirls flashed   and animal rights   yardies mashed throats gashed

and Nazi whites   rooms trashed   Giro cashed   and love bites   acid splashed

mistress lashed   and ugly sites   this is UK living   pick up a brochure

today   teens stare at screen glare   attackers tear underwear   kids on e's

divorcees   vandalised trees   backstreet sleaze   speed kills   sleeping pills

nil nils   and road drills   access snags   for weekend dads   with carrier bags

nomads   schoolgirl sex pest   undressed confessed this is UK living

non stop Brit pop   corner shops and bus stops   wife beaters   happy eaters

sun seekers   cheap heaters   Bovis homes   Cellnet phones   Top Man clones

no-go zones   head butts   at Pizza Hut   shops shut   and Silk Cut   freemasons

dark locations   Waynes and Jasons   timewasters   cheap brands   wastelands

tribute bands   cheap scams   Cash Converters   factory shirkers   wife deserters

and loadsa flirters   shelf stackers   chicken packers   cb hackers   christmas

crackers this is UK living   crap settees   quick decrees   legal fees   Rennie Rapeze

highchairs   pushchairs   despair and welfare   take a leaflet   soft porn   hard porn

popcorn   and overdrawn   and while I think about it   fuck off the CSA

wife swappers   bent coppers   tennieboppers and blowjobbers   faith healers

straight tequilas   class A dealers   and vice squeelers   human zoo   neck tattoes

Spar shampoo   and kung foo   benefit aid   underpaid   flagging trade   and another

200 layed off in Essex   this is UK living   Liam Gallagher was Prime Minister and Gazza

was laying down face up at Wembley   and Alison you were the most fantstic woman

in my lifetime   I will never forget you   tabloids   steroids   androids and the

unemployed   tinsel trash   pie and mash   pebble dash   culture clash   empty souls

digging holes   bacon rolls   barbie dolls   junk mail   cons on bail   cons in jail

clearance sales   battered whore   on the floor   holding score   breaking law

drunk drivers   dare devil riders   deep sea divers   and neck spiders   Avon janes

with ankle chains   in bowling lanes   empty brains   crow bars   low cars   loadsa jars

under pars   kids at raves   microwaves   low paid slaves   supersaves   lover grips

silicone tits   curvey bits   and rips Ann Summers wear off while watching Match of

the Day at a 3 bed semi in South Woodham Ferrers   this is near Chelmsford in

Essex in case anyone was wondering   love bites   pub fights   cheap tights   building

sites   cd roms   video comms   protection from peeping toms   lonely hearts

after dark   look for tarts   and spare parts   wash and go   dosh and blow cosh and go

and run down the road like fuck   block pathing   insider trading   sun bathing

and parading yer flash BMW   suicide blondes   local cons   and another youth

absconds with a handbag on Southend sea front   this is UK living   circa   june 1996

I know because I was there and I saw it   tyres slashed   and windscreen smashed

Cindy Beals   deals on wheels   Grants and Phils   like Cathy's Meals   paper trips

bags of chips   lipseal lips   and hidden whips   attitudes   frozen food   family feuds

fashions crude   and many hair styles were crude too   legal disputes   money disputes

homes uproot   decree absolute   pulp fiction   Hygena Kitchens   council petitions

drug addition   bingo halls   lottery balls   artex walls and trinket stalls   jailbait

on blind dates   love fakes   heartaches   sticks of rock   aimless flocks   concrete

blocks and digital clocks   kids invade   penny arcades   in designer shades with

silver blades   out on the A12 early on a Saturday morning in June 1996

fox splattered   litter scattered   windscreens shattered   panels battered   a Texas

landscape   ugly shapes   Planet of the Apes   scene of rapes   pneumatic drills

headache pills   standstills   a treadmill   stuck on tarmac   in a tailback   waiting for

a rage attack   power lines   freak designs   and Frankenstiens   and so

eventually back to the delights of a market town   sheep   more sheep   and pigs

detector vans   lager cans   ultra violet tans   and one night stands   tonight and

every night   this is UK living   Big Macs and baseball caps   everywhere

you look   unpaid tax and suicide pacts   the ghosts of mods and rockers at funerals